EXTREME WEATHER JOBS

HOTSHOT CREWS

BY ASHLEY GISH

WWW.APEXEDITIONS.COM

Apex is distributed by North Star Editions:
sales@northstareditions.com | 888-417-0195

Produced for Apex by Red Line Editorial.

Photographs ©: Rich Pedroncelli/AP Images, cover; Percy Jones/DVIDS, 1, 24; Kyle Miller/Wyoming Hotshots/USFS, 4–5; Shutterstock Images, 6, 8, 15, 19, 29; iStockphoto, 7, 14, 20–21, 22–23, 25; Pacific Southwest Forest Service/USDA, 10–11, 18; Mark J. Terrill/AP Images, 12–13; Charity Parks/USDA, 16–17; Andrew Hostad/Southwestern Region/USFS, 26–27

Library of Congress Control Number: 2023921621

ISBN
978-1-63738-917-1 (hardcover)
978-1-63738-957-7 (paperback)
979-8-89250-053-1 (ebook pdf)
979-8-89250-015-9 (hosted ebook)

Printed in the United States of America
Mankato, MN
082024

NOTE TO PARENTS AND EDUCATORS

Apex books are designed to build literacy skills in striving readers. Exciting, high-interest content attracts and holds readers' attention. The text is carefully leveled to allow students to achieve success quickly. Additional features, such as bolded glossary words for difficult terms, help build comprehension.

TABLE OF CONTENTS

CHAPTER 1

HOTSHOT HEROES

A wildfire rages through the forest. A team of hotshots gets ready to fight it. They grab their chainsaws and backpacks.

Hotshots fight large fires that burn forests and other natural areas.

Fire lines are strips of bare ground. They help slow wildfires.

The fire destroys everything in its path. But the hotshots have a plan. They clear away **brush** to make a fire line. They dig **trenches** around the fire.

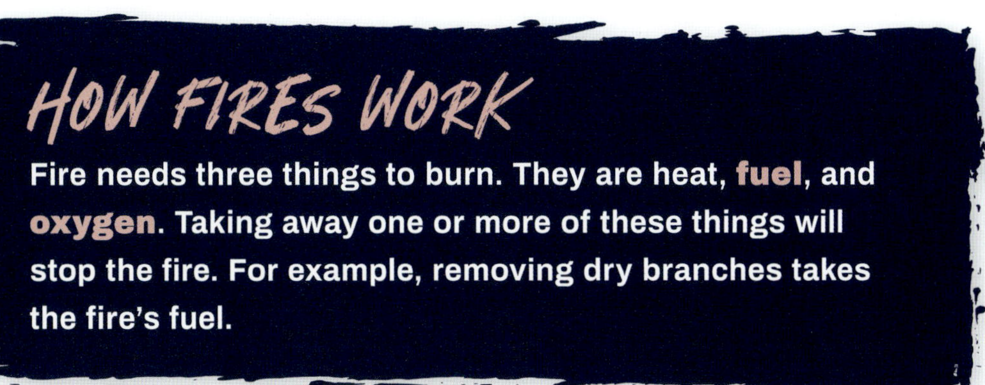

HOW FIRES WORK

Fire needs three things to burn. They are heat, **fuel**, and **oxygen**. Taking away one or more of these things will stop the fire. For example, removing dry branches takes the fire's fuel.

Small trees and dead branches catch fire easily. They provide fuel that helps wildfires spread.

The flames reach the fire line. But they can't spread past it. The hotshots watch to make sure the fire is **contained**. They keep the rest of the forest safe.

A large wildfire may take many days to contain.

CHAPTER 2

HOTSHOT HISTORY

Hotshots go to the hottest parts of wildfires. They work to put the fires out. The first hotshot teams formed in the 1940s. They fought wildfires in California.

The Laguna Hotshots were one of the first crews in the United States. The team still fights fires today.

Early hotshots were very good at their jobs. So, more teams formed. By the 1980s, hotshots were working in several US states.

FAST FACT

Deanne Shulman was the first woman to become a hotshot. She was hired in 1976.

In the 1990s, hotshots in all states began to go through the same training.

Today there are more than 100 hotshot teams throughout the United States. They often work in **remote** areas. They help save land from wildfire damage.

Several wildfires have burned in Big Cypress National Preserve. This natural area is in Florida.

Wildfires are becoming stronger and more common throughout the United States.

WILD WEST

Wildfires can happen anywhere. But they're most common in western states. These states include California and Nevada. They often have **droughts**, dry plants, and hot **climates**.

CHAPTER 3

TRAINING AND GEAR

Hotshots have a very dangerous job. So, they need **specialized** training. The training takes weeks to complete.

Hotshots may spend many days working far from cities or towns.

Hotshots train to carry about 40 pounds (18 kg) of gear.

Most of the training is physical. Hotshots must be able to run fast and far. And they must be able to carry everything they need to fight a fire.

Hotshots may use GPS devices to help find their way in the wilderness.

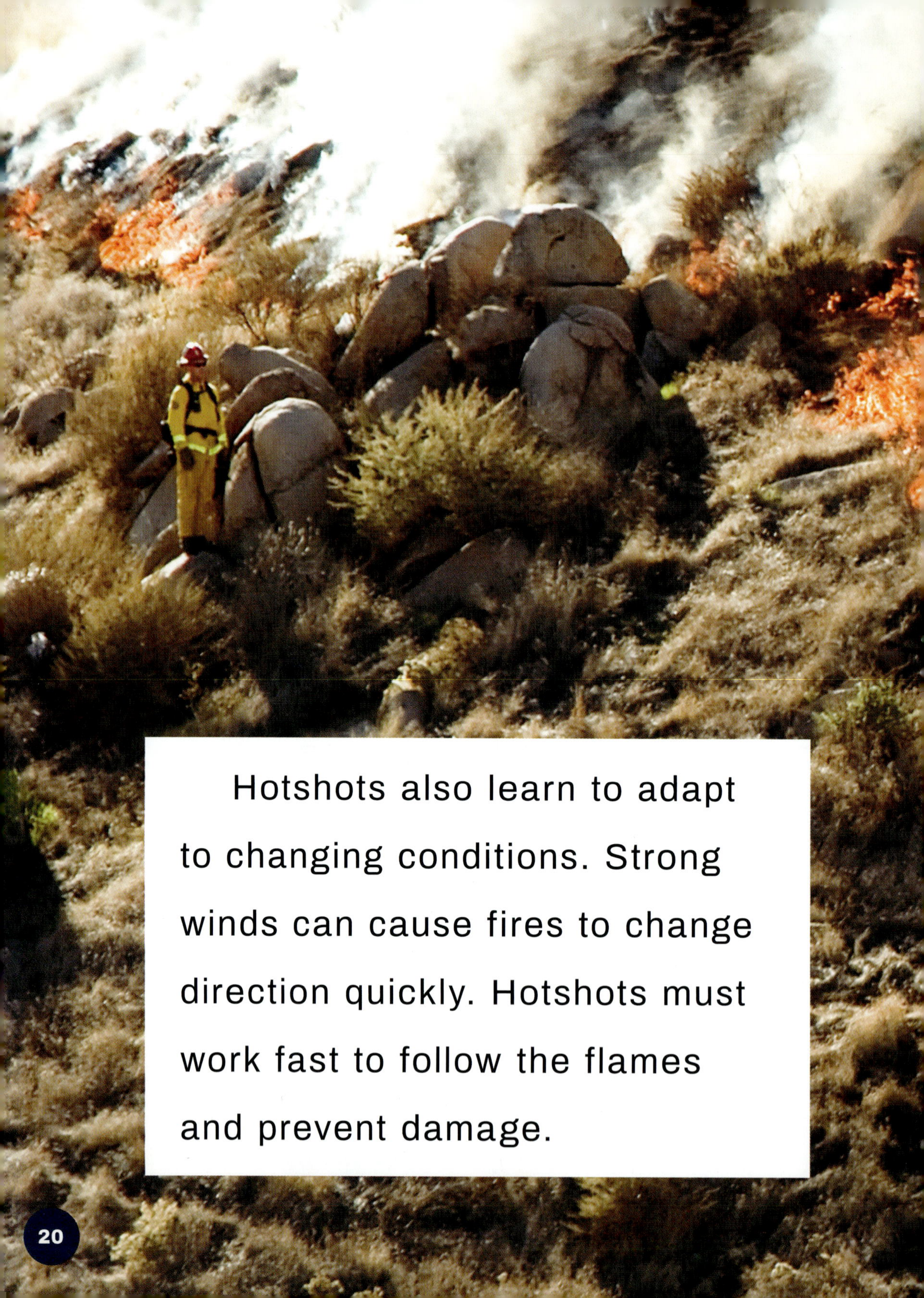

Hotshots also learn to adapt to changing conditions. Strong winds can cause fires to change direction quickly. Hotshots must work fast to follow the flames and prevent damage.

TRAINED TO SAVE

Some wildfires get close to places where people live. Hotshots stop the fires from reaching homes and businesses. They are also trained to protect people.

Hotshots often work in areas that are hard to reach.

CHAPTER 4

ON THE JOB

Hotshot teams are on call during fire season. This means they may be called to a job at any time.

Fire season is the time of year when wildfires are most common. It lasts for several months.

Hotshots may travel many miles to reach fires. They often take trucks or planes. They set up a camp. Hotshots stay until the fire is under control. They may work 16 hours a day.

Sometimes hotshots travel by helicopter.

Hotshots often sleep in tents or on the ground.

FAST FACT

Hotshot crews may have to work for more than 100 days in one fire season.

Hotshots often face smoke and blazing heat. Clothes and boots made of strong materials help them stay safe. Hotshots also carry fire shelters. These sheets protect hotshots if a fire gets too close.

GETTING AHEAD

Hotshots work ahead to slow wildfires. Sometimes they burn an area on purpose. This removes fuel. When fire reaches the burned area, it can't grow or spread.

People wrap fire shelters around their bodies to help block the flames.

COMPREHENSION QUESTIONS

Write your answers on a separate piece of paper.

1. Write a few sentences describing the main ideas of Chapter 2.

2. Would you want to be a hotshot firefighter? Why or why not?

3. How many hotshots are on most teams?

- **A.** fewer than 13
- **B.** about 20
- **C.** more than 100

4. How could dry plants make wildfires more likely?

- **A.** Dry plants cannot grow.
- **B.** Dry plants cannot burn.
- **C.** Dry plants can catch fire easily.

5. What does **physical** mean in this book?

Most of the training is ***physical****. Hotshots must be able to run fast and far.*

A. using the body
B. using the mind
C. using many tools

6. What does **conditions** mean in this book?

Hotshots also learn to adapt to changing ***conditions****. Strong winds can cause fires to change direction quickly.*

A. types of weather
B. names of places
C. kinds of animals

Answer key on page 32.

GLOSSARY

brush

Small trees and bushes.

climates

The usual weather in certain areas.

contained

Kept within a set area.

droughts

Times of little or no rain.

fuel

Material, such as wood, that can burn and release heat.

oxygen

A gas in the air. Animals need oxygen to breathe, and fires need it to burn.

remote

Far away from towns or people.

specialized

Involving extra focus, skill, or training.

trenches

Long, narrow ditches dug into the ground.

BOOKS

Mattern, Joanne. *Wildfires*. Minneapolis: Kaleidoscope, 2023.

Potenza, Alessandra. *All About Wildfires*. New York: Children's Press, 2021.

Ransom, Candice. *Wildfires*. Mendota Heights, MN: Apex Editions, 2023.

ONLINE RESOURCES

Visit **www.apexeditions.com** to find links and resources related to this title.

ABOUT THE AUTHOR

Ashley Gish has authored more than 60 juvenile nonfiction books. She lives in Minnesota.

INDEX

ANSWER KEY:

1. Answers will vary; 2. Answers will vary; 3. B; 4. C; 5. A; 6. A